Odd & Unusual BEDFORDSHIRE

by
Alan Cox

CONSERVATION SECTION, PLANNING DEPARTMENT
BEDFORDSHIRE COUNTY COUNCIL

Illustrations by John Johnson

A Nuclear Free Zone

Graphics by the County Planning Department
Phototypeset in Souvenir by Bedfordshire County Council Reprographics Unit
Printed by Bedfordshire County Council Reprographics Unit

Foreword

A few years ago my predecessor, Geoffrey Cowley, had the idea for an illustrated talk on "Odd & Unusual Bedfordshire". It has proved extremely popular, and both he and, latterly, Alan Cox have given this talk to countless local groups. In response to many requests we have now produced the book of the talk, as it were. The text has been written by Alan Cox with suggestions from David Baker, Stewart Cuff, Liz Marten, and Angela Simco. Most of the drawings are based on photographs taken by Ken Whitbread and Dave Stubbs of the County Council's Photographic Unit.

A.M. Griffin
County Planning Officer

Introduction

There are always those fascinating oddities which are only known to a handful of locals: a quaint survival from the past perhaps, or an exhuberant decorative detail; and eccentric structure put up at the whim of a rich patron, or something which has an unusual story attached to it. The rest of us have to discover such things by chance and even then we may not be aware of their true significance. For this reason the present publication offers a selection of what we have called "Odd and Unusual Bedfordshire" and gives, where possible, some details of the history or background of each item. While it is not intended primarily as a guide-book, readers may want to see for themselves many of the things mentioned, and to make this easier six-figure map references are given in brackets. Although almost all the items are visible from public roads or footpaths, a number stand on private property, and the rights of owners and occupiers should be respected.

We have not included a contents page because we feel that readers may enjoy the surprise of discovering for themselves what is depicted in these pages. However, for guidance a map showing the places described is included.

We hope that the things in this booklet will not be dismissed as little more than whimsical curiosities. In an increasingly stereotyped world their preservation is no longer a mere luxury — it has now become a necessity if some character and individuality is to be retained. Looking at them costs nothing at all, but repair and maintenance often costs a great deal of money; if we are happy to pay substantial entrance fees to visit country houses, should we not be equally prepared to contribute to the preservation of such things as dovecotes, lock-ups, or parish pumps? If we are not, they will become extinct as the dinosaur or the dodo, and we shall have deprived future generations of the pleasures we ourselves have enjoyed.

Odd & Unusual BEDFORDSHIRE

Index Map

Cast-iron milestone made about 1891, now at Peartree Cottage, High Street, Sharnbrook; the last surviving example in the county.

Luton

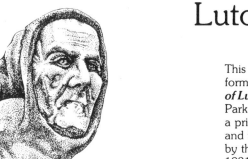

This strange creature, half-animal, half-human forms a decorative **terra-cotta crest to the roof of Luton Museum and Art Gallery** in Wardown Park (TL 089229). The museum was built as a private house for a local solicitor in 1875 and together with the grounds was acquired by the town in 1904, becoming a museum in 1931.

The porte-cochere, or carriage-porch, which protects the front door of the museum is also adorned with **terra-cotta busts of distinguished Victorians.** Here Benjamin Disraeli, one of the most famous of all British Prime Ministers, is portrayed on the right while Charles Dickens, the equally famous novelist, is shown on the left. The other notables represented on the porch are Palmerston, Gladstone, Cobden, and Bright.

1

Luton

Alongside the east side of Luton Museum is the only surviving **hexagonal Victorian post box** in the county. It is now simply an open air exhibit but once stood near Luton Town Hall. Such six-sided pillar boxes are known as "Penfolds" after the man who designed them, J.W. Penfold, and the type was introduced in 1866. Although a very elegant design, the hexagonal pillar box had practical difficulties not the least of which was that the mail tended to get caught up and trapped in all the corners. This led to it being superseded from 1879 by cylindrical pillar boxes.

Kempston

This **pillar box in Spring Road, Kempston** (TL 039480) is an example of one of the earliest types of cylindrical post box introduced in 1879. It is known as an "Anonymous" box because it was not until 1887 that somebody pointed out to the Post Office that they had forgotten to put on the royal cypher and coat-of-arms, or even the words "Post Office". The GPO hastily introduced a new type of cylindrical box bearing the VR cypher.

Stevington

In the days before piped water, springs and wells were of great importance and were often endued with magical or religious associations, especially curative powers. The **Holy Well at Stevington** (SP 990536), set in a recess in the boundary wall of the churchyard, was a place of pilgrimage in the Middle Ages. As late as the last century it was being used for washing sheep, and the ancient spring which still feeds it has never been known to freeze or run dry.

Turvey

On an island in the River Great Ouse stand Bedfordshire's "Odd Couple", *Jonah and his wife, beside the bridge at Turvey* (SP 938523).

Jonah originally stood in the quadrangle of Ashbridge House, Hertfordshire, placed there, so it is said, in the early 18th century by the 1st Earl of Bridgewater. In 1802, when the old house was pulled down, the statue was sold off and after several years it turned up in the yard of a Bedford stonemason, where it was seen by the squire of Turvey, John Higgins. He bought it and placed it in its present position in 1844.

There is no real reason to suppose that the statue is actually meant to be Jonah, for the fish at his feet appears to be a dolphin rather than a whale, but the nickname is now too well established ever to be changed.

Jonah's "wife" is even more dubious. She only joined him in 1953 and is a very strange lady indeed – an obviously female body with a bearded head! Her body was found by the then owner of Turvey Mill built into the partially collapsed wall of a barn, together with several miscellaneous heads, the best preserved of which was selected.

Totternhoe

The most remarkable watermill in the county is **Doolittle Mill, Totternhoe** (SP 990201). For it is a combined wind and watermill, one of only twelve examples known in the whole country. The buildings probably date from the early 19th century although there has been a mill on or near the site for centuries. The top and sails of the windmill blew off in a storm about 1880 but the mill still continued to be worked by water, supplemented by a steam-engine, until the 1920s. The waterwheel has now largely disappeared but much of the machinery still survives inside the mill. Incidentally, the name "Doolittle" is often given to the upper-most mill on a stream, in this case the River Ouzel, since frequently there was insufficient water to turn its wheel, and hence the need for a windmill as well.

Haynes

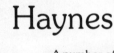

A number of other parish pumps are to be seen in local villages and this is a particularly ornate **pump at Haynes Church End** (TL 082411). Its carved wooden case bears a suitable text and the metal spout is in the form of a medieval gargoyle. Protection is afforded by a pretty wooden shelter with a decorative tiled roof. The whole thing was put up about 1867 by Lord John Thynne and no doubt much of its picturesque appearance is due to the fact that it stands opposite the entrance to what was his country house, Hawnes Park (now Clarendon School).

Ampthill

This combined *pump, signpost, and lamp standard on Ampthill Market Place* (TL 034381) is in the form of an elegant stone obelisk. As the inscription around the base records, it was erected by the Earl of Upper Ossory in 1785 and was designed by the well-known architect, Sir William Chambers. Unfortunately, all that remains of the lamp is an iron socket at the top, but there are plans to put back a copy. At the foot of each face of the obelisk, the distance is given to an important town in that direction (Bedford, Woburn, Dunstable, and London respectively).

Heath & Reach

Even more substantial is the brick-built *wellhouse and clock tower on Heath Green, Heath and Reach* (SP 925280), erected by subscription in 1873. The cost of the clock was borne by Baroness Burdett Coutts and Baroness de Rothschild, while the pump was presented by Mr Brantom in memory of William Abraham. These details are recorded on three inscribed stones set into the building. Through the iron grilles of the wellhouse can still be seen the four foot diameter wheel that was used to draw water.

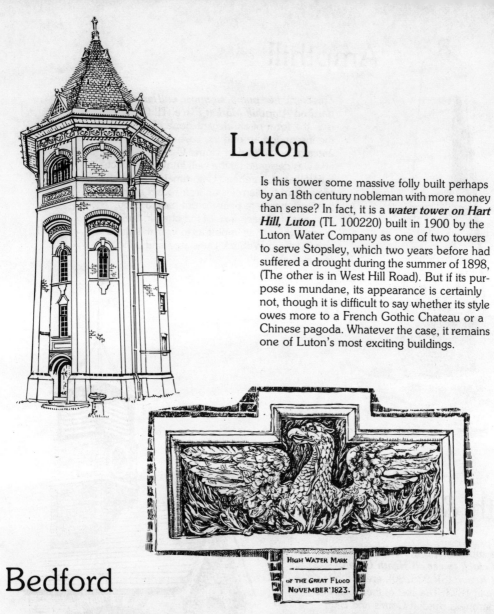

Luton

Is this tower some massive folly built perhaps by an 18th century nobleman with more money than sense? In fact, it is a *water tower on Hart Hill, Luton* (TL 100220) built in 1900 by the Luton Water Company as one of two towers to serve Stopsley, which two years before had suffered a drought during the summer of 1898, (The other is in West Hill Road). But if its purpose is mundane, its appearance is certainly not, though it is difficult to say whether its style owes more to a French Gothic Chateau or a Chinese pagoda. Whatever the case, it remains one of Luton's most exciting buildings.

HIGH WATER MARK
OF THE GREAT FLOOD
NOVEMBER 1823.

Bedford

Sometimes you can have to much water and in November 1823 the River Ouse burst its banks, causing massive floods. The event is recorded by inscription on Oakly Bridge and the Three Fyshes public house at Turvey, as well as this *flood level on the Phoenix Public*

House, St. John's Street, Bedford (TL 051491). The extent of the flooding can be judged by the fact that this mark is about a quarter of a mile from the river. Above, a terracotta panel depicting a phoenix rising from the flames, makes a distinctive pub sign.

Bedford

Horses have long ceased to drink from this cast-iron **horse-trough in Kempston Road, Bedford** (TL 042486) and now it serves as an unwilling receptacle for people's litter. It bears a plate proclaiming the fact that it was Presented to the Borough by Amelia, widow of J.B., A Friend of Dumb Animals, April 1895. Who J.B. was, we have been unable to discover, but no doubt the dumb animals were suitably grateful to him; not only the horses but also the dogs who were provided with a small trough at one end of the base.

Linslade

This building looks for all the world like an eskimo's igloo in brick. The comparison is not very far from the truth, for it is an **ice house in the garden of The Lodge, Bossington Lane, Linslade** (SP 917259). In the days before refrigerators ice would be cut from a nearby frozen lake or pond during the winter and stored in this ice house. Then in summer, blocks of ice would be removed to the kitchen of the big house (now demolished) to store things like fish and meat, or to prepare ice cream and other delicacies. Much of the ice house is set below ground in order to provide insulation and prevent the ice from melting.

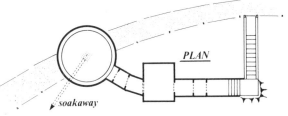

PLAN

soakaway

Silsoe

This can be seen in the plan of the rather more elaborate **ice house at Wrest Park, Silsoe** (TL 087365), which may date from about 1673, but is not accessible to the public. Many of the more substantial houses in the county had such ice houses in their grounds and they were used from the second half of the 17th century until the early years of the present century.

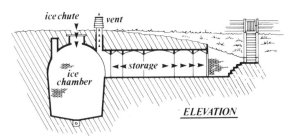

ice chute *vent*

ice chamber

◄◄ *storage* ►►►

ELEVATION

Willington

It was a medieval privilege that only the lord of the manor could keep pigeons; they provided him with fresh meat and eggs in winter as an alternative to interminable salted beef or pork, while their droppings made an excellent fertilizer. All this was obtained at no expense to the lord himself since the pigeons happily fed off the crops and seed of his tenants – a subtle form of feudal indirect taxation!

One can imagine, therefore, how the tenants groaned when they saw the completion of the enormous stone-built **Tudor dovecote at Willington** (TL 107499). It was built by Sir John Gostwick, who was an official to Cardinal Wolsey but had the sense to transfer his allegiance to King Henry VIII and was able to purchase the manor of Willington in 1529. His manor house has largely disappeared, but the dovecote together with the adjacent stable-block are now maintained by the National Trust and are occasionally open to the public on summer weekends. It is well worth trying to see inside the dovecote, for the interior is an amazing sight with row upon row of square nesting boxes for the birds, some 1,500 boxes in all.

Old Warden

The **Swiss Garden, Old Warden** (TL 149446) is a charming eight acre garden, probably laid out in the 1820s and 1830s by the 3rd Lord Ongley, with alterations and additions by the Shuttleworths who bought the Old Warden estate in the 1870s. It contains bridges, walk-ways, statues, a grotto, and various buildings including the *Swiss Cottage,* shown here, which gives the whole garden its name. It is said that Lord Ongley had a Swiss mistress who lived in this cottage, but if she did it must have been very draughty and uncomfortable for it is only a summerhouse. The legend goes on that she and Lord Ongley had a son who died at the age of about nine, and that an uninscribed stone cross, still surviving in the garden marks his grave. Some years ago, under the Shuttleworths, the gardeners began to hear voices and feel presences. It turned out that when tidying up part of the garden they had moved the cross; it was hastily returned to its old spot and there have been no more disturbances. After years of neglect the garden and its features are slowly being restored by the County Council, who have leased it and have made it accessible to the public at certain times.

Aspley Guise

Humphrey Repton, the famous landscape architect, designed **Henry VII Lodge, Aspley Guise** (SP 931352), about 1811, for the 6th Duke of Bedford. It stands just to the north of Woburn Sands crossroads, on the east side of the road to Woburn. Apart from its picturesque appearance the Lodge is an interesting attempt to recreate a perfect late 15th century house copying details from authentic examples. Repton himself tells us that:

The hint of the lower storey was taken from Eltham Palace, the hints for the brick-nogging from a house at King's Lynn, for the arches at the top of the narrow panels from a house at Shrewsbury, for the oriel from Norwich, and for the chimneys from Wollerton Manor House, Barsham, Norfolk.

Haynes

Art imitates nature: an intricate wrought-iron sunflower makes a splendid finial on the gable of the Victorian **lodge to Hawnes Park** (now Clarendon School) at Haynes Church End (TL 082411). It stands opposite the pump mentioned earlier and was probably built about the same time. There is also an inscription in French running around the lodge on a band above the ground-floor windows.

Eversholt

These **Bedford Estate cottages, Water End, Eversholt** (SP 988336) were built in 1907 by Herbrand, the 11th Duke of Bedford. Similar groups dating from the early years of this century are to be found in other Bedford Estate villages. The odd thing is that there are no front doors, only back ones. It is said that the Duke did not like to see women gossiping at their front doors and this was his way of making sure they did not do so. However, this may well be unfair to the Duke who was so short-sighted that he would probably never have noticed what they were doing anyway.

Woburn

It was also the 11th Duke of Bedford who had part of the immense **brick wall round Woburn Park** rebuilt about 1900. The renewed section runs alongside the road between Ridgmont and Woburn, from the lodge gates on the edge of Ridgmont (SP 957357) round to the next lodge gates at Husborne Crawley (SP 957351). A closer look reveals that the bricks of some of the buttresses have gone rusty. In fact the buttresses are cast-iron incised to look like brickwork, and it is said that the Duke bought them to save a friend who owned an ironworks from bankruptcy. Actually the buttresses serve a very practical purpose, for they are hollow; this allows for expansion or contraction, which if the wall had been built in one continuous length would have caused the wall to buckle, then crack, and finally collapse.

Ampthill

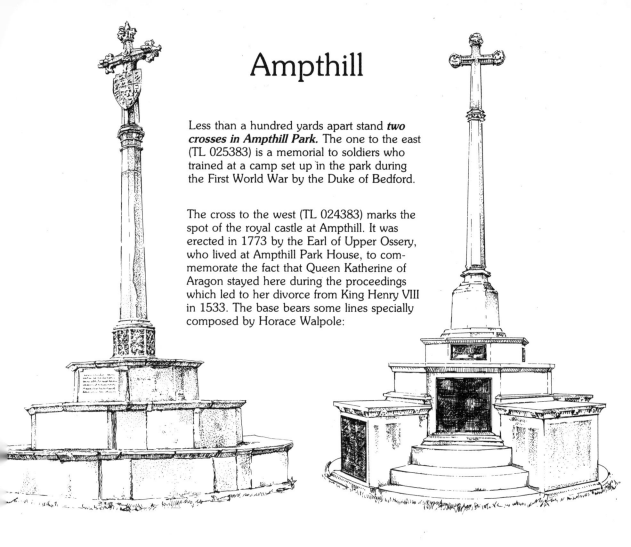

Less than a hundred yards apart stand **two crosses in Ampthill Park.** The one to the east (TL 025383) is a memorial to soldiers who trained at a camp set up in the park during the First World War by the Duke of Bedford.

The cross to the west (TL 024383) marks the spot of the royal castle at Ampthill. It was erected in 1773 by the Earl of Upper Ossery, who lived at Ampthill Park House, to commemorate the fact that Queen Katherine of Aragon stayed here during the proceedings which led to her divorce from King Henry VIII in 1533. The base bears some lines specially composed by Horace Walpole:

In days of old, here Ampthill's Towers were seen,
The mournful refuge of an injured queen;
Here flowed her pure but unavailing tears,
Here blinded zeal sustained her sinking years.
Yet Freedom hence her radiant banner waved,
And love avenged a realm by priests enslaved;
From Katherine's wrongs a Nation's bliss was spread
And Luther's light from Henry's lawless bed.

Evidently Walpole did not intend to let his obvious sympathy for the queen dampen his Whig enthusiasm for the Protestant Reformation.

Ampthill

Local legend also associates Queen Katherine with this elegant *triangular gazebo in Dunstable Street, Ampthill* (TL 034379). The story is that during her time in Ampthill it was here that the queen taught the art of pillow lacemaking to Bedfordshire women. Whether or not the queen was actually responsible for introducing lacemaking into this area, is a matter of conjecture, but we can be sure that she never as much as set foot in this summerhouse, since it was not built until the 18th century, long after her death.

Not far from the gazebo is another reminder of a royal personality. A *wall-painting inside the White Hart Hotel, Ampthill* (TL 034380), was recently discovered during alterations, after having been concealed for over 300 years. It shows the rose, the thistle, and in the centre the plume of feathers of the Prince of Wales, together with the date 1646. The Prince of Wales in question was, therefore, the future Charles II, at this time seeking refuge on the Continent because, of course, this was during the English Civil War. It is not known who put this painting here but it was probably hastily covered over when Charles I finally lost both the war and his head. Because of this, it is still in remarkably good condition and can be seen during normal licensing hours.

Toddington

Up until at least the 17th century there was still a common belief in witchcraft, and anything abnormal tended to be explained in terms of witches. Thus **Conger Hill, Toddington** (TL 011288), a flat-topped mound to the east of the parish church, is probably the remains of a medieval castle, but popular imagination transformed it into the lair of a witch. Every Shrove Tuesday the children of the village assemble on Conger Hill and at the first stroke of twelve noon they put their ears to the ground to hear the witch's pancakes sizzling. As with many other customs, this is an odd mixture of christian and pagan beliefs.

Marston Moretaine

Another favourite explanation for something abnormal, or otherwise unexplained, was that it must have been the work of the Devil. An example is the so-called **"Devil's Toenail"** or **"Devil's Jump Stone" at Marston Moretaine** (SP 999408). This is an old stone about three foot high, situated to the south of the village in a field on the east side of the road to Lidlington. Once there were three such stones across the fields here and legend has it that these stones indicated a series of jumps made by the Devil, although there are at least two versions of what he was doing at the time. One story is that the surviving stone marks the spot of one of the Devil's jumps when he was trying to carry off the church tower; in the event the tower proved too heavy for him and he left it in its present position separated from the main body of the church. The other version of the

legend has it that a former owner of the field where the stone stands was playing at "jumps" or leap-frog on the Sabbath when the Devil jumped down from the church, landing on the spot marked by the stone. He siezed the wretched man and leapt away with him into eternity.

Shillington

These odd marks appear to the right of the door of an otherwise straightforward early 17th century timber-framed house. They represent manacles and this is the **Old Court House at Apsley End, Shillington** (TL 119322), where the local Justices of the Peace met to deal with petty cases.

Clophill

No doubt some of those who appeared before the Justices had spent the previous night in the parish lock-up or cage. The **lock-up and pound at Clophill** (TL 082376) dates from the 19th century and stands beside the green. The pound is the walled enclosure on the right where any animals found straying in the parish were impounded until their owners paid a fine to get them back.

Harrold

Other lock-ups survive at Blunham, Silsoe and Turvey, but architecturally speaking the best remaining example in the county is this **lock-up on the Green at Harrold** (SP 951567). In spite of its primitive form it was only put up in 1824. Although it may now look like a charming relic of the past, the stout door and complete absence of windows must have made a night spent here a very unpleasant experience.

Also to be found on the green is **Harrold market-house** (SP 951567) erected in the early 18th century. Its roof, supported by eight wooden posts and surmounted by a cupola, sheltered some of the stall-holders, especially those selling more perishable goods like dairy produce; hence it is sometimes referred to as the *Butter-Cross*.

Dunstable

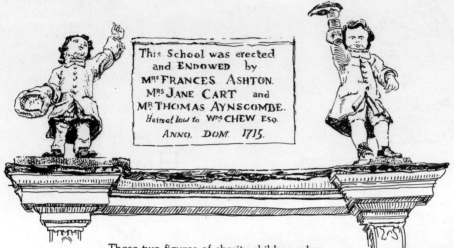

> This School was erected
> and ENDOWED by
> Mrs FRANCES ASHTON.
> Mrs JANE CART and
> Mr THOMAS AYNSCOMBE.
> Heirs at law to Wm CHEW Esq.
> ANNO. DOM. 1715.

These two figures of charity children adorn the front of **Chew's School, High Street South, Dunstable** (TL 021216), although the building is now put to local community use. William Chew was a successful London distiller and as the inscription records the school was built and endowed in his memory in 1715. It was intended for forty boys all of whom had to be members of the Church of England. Next door are the almshouses built a few years later by Chew's daughter, Mrs Jane Cart.

Ickwell Green

The village green is a favourite place for celebrating May Day, but few villages can rival the fine red and white striped **maypole on Ickwell Green** (TL 149455). Written records show that May Day celebrations have been taking place on the green at Ickwell since at least 1563 and a permanent maypole was first erected here in 1872, although the present maypole is a modern replacement.

Broom

One of the most striking groups of almshouses in Bedfordshire is the **Fordham Almshouses in High Street, Broom** (TL 172430). This row of three dwellings was built in 1913 in memory of Janet Fordham by her husband, Rupert, who lived at Broom Hall at the time. The curving roofs and porches, combined with stone walls that look like crazy-paving, produce a slightly surrealist appearance.

Clifton

This diminutive building, in spite of its smallness and the fact that there is only one central window, is actually a pair of almshouses. The **"Gleaner and Sower" beside the road at Clifton** (TL 163389) owe their origin to Septimus Sears, the first minister of Clifton's Strict and Particular Baptist Chapel. During the thirty-five years of his ministry he edited and promoted the sale of various religious tracts, including the monthly magazines, *The Little Gleaner for the Young* and *The Sower*. In 1871 he appealed to the readers of these two periodicals for money toward the building of a pair of almshouses for widows. Hence there is an inscription above either doorway, one reading *Gleaner and Sower* and the other *Widows Homes*. After a period of neglect the building, although no longer an almshouse, has been converted to a single dwelling with the minimum of external alteration.

Roxton

Most Noncomformist chapels have a sober classical facade so the mock rustic cottage-ornee style of the **thatched Congregational Chapel at Roxton** (TL 151544) comes as a surprise. The local squire, Charles Metcalfe, was a Congregationalist and getting tired of having to travel six miles to the nearest chapel, he decided to build a chapel on the edge of his estate at Roxton in 1808. Because it could be seen from his house, he decided that it might as well be picturesque to look at, so that in addition to the thatched roof it has ogee-pointed windows and a twisted tree trunk verandah. There is even a small summerhouse set in the back corner, intended for the private use of the Metcalfe family.

Leighton Buzzard

This amusing **graffito in All Saints Church, Leighton Buzzard** (SP 918248), is scratched on the south-west crossing pier. This medieval couple are known as Simon and Nellie, and they are squabbling over whether the Mothering Sunday cake should be boiled or baked. Nellie seems to have got very heated and is attacking her husband with a ladle, but eventually they agreed to compromise by cooking the cake both ways.

Eaton Bray

For centuries the parish church was the only substantial public building in most communities and so it was used for all sorts of purposes. For example it was customary to ring the church bells backwards to indicate a fire and any fire-fighting equipment would be kept in the church. A few relics can still be found such as the set

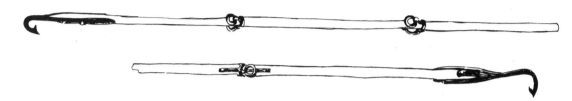

of leather buckets in Northill Church and the two **firehooks in St Mary's Church, Eaton Bray** (SP 969207). They were used to remove thatch from burning roofs or to pull down a timber-framed building to create a fire-break and prevent the spread of a major fire.

Cople

On the front lawn of a modern house is what looks like a rather elaborate garden shed. In fact this was the **parish bier house at Cople** (TL 103485), built in the late 19th century to store the bier on which coffins were wheeled into the church for funerals. Because of a change of land-ownership, the occupier of the new house found himself with this unusual adjunct to his property. Fortunately he was sympathetic to its retention and with a grant from the County Council it has been fully restored.

Riseley

Here is a very odd sight two **gravestones on the roadside at Keysoe Road, Riseley** (TL 042628). The grass verge where they stand was once the site of the burial ground of the Baptist Chapel and these were the only two stones in it. The chapel was demolished in the 1960s but the gravestones have been left.

Tilsworth

A sad and sinister story is told on a **gravestone in Tilsworth churchyard** (SP 975242). It reads:

This stone was erected by subscription to the memory of a female unknown found murdered in Blackgrove Wood August 15, 1821.

> *Oh pause my friends and drop the silent tear*
> *Attend and learn why I was buried here;*
> *Perchance some distant earth had hid my clay*
> *If I'd outlived the sad, the fatal day;*
> *To you unknown, my case not understood*
> *From whence I came or why in Blackgrove Wood.*
> *This truth's too clear and nearly all that's known,*
> *I there was murdered and the villains flown.*
> *May god whose piercing eye pursues his flight*
> *Pardon the crime but bring the deed to light.*

But the murderers were never caught, and the victim has never been identified.

Bedford

This **gravestone in St Paul's Churchyard, Bedford** (TL 050496) is now becoming worn but it records the death in 1717 of the wife of Shadrach Johnson. She gave birth to 12 sons and 12 daughters, a remarkable feat considering, as the inscription shows, she was only 38 when she died. She must have spent virtually the whole of her married life in confinement. No wonder the poor woman's name was Patience!

Bedford

On St Paul's Square, Bedford, stands the **statue of John Howard** (TL 050496). The famous Bedfordshire-based prison reformer died in 1790 and just over a hundred years later in 1894 a statue was erected in his honour. The figure is conventional enough but around the base is a flowing Art Nouveau design in bronze with grotesque masks at the corners. A closer look reveals that peering out from behind these masks are little babes – presumably symbolizing that however corrupt a person may seem, a certain inner innocence still remains. The sculptor of both statue and base was Sir Alfred Gilbert whose most famous work is the statue of Eros in Piccadilly Circus.

JOHN HOWARD

Bedford

While shop-fronts are usually modern, the facades above them may be much older. For example, the upper storeys of what is now **Dunn's, 57 High Street, Bedford** (TL 050497) were designed in a neo-Gothic style in 1871 by the Bedford architect, John Usher. The pinnacles at the top are surmounted by gun dogs modelled by the Exeter sculptor, Harry Hems, and they are a reminder that this was once the shop of a gun-smith, Henry Adkins, whose initials can be seen above the central second-floor window.

A few doors down is the most prominent sign in the street, the **golden bull and clock above 49 High Street, Bedford** (TL 050497). It was put there in 1884 by John Bull and Company whose jeweller's shop occupied these premises until they moved to another site in the town in 1964. Luckily the clock has been retained although the bull is a fibreglass copy of the original wooden one which has been removed to Bedford Museum.

Leighton Buzzard

Unfortunately, many individualistic signs have given way to sterotyped neon ones and plastic lettering. So it is nice to see the attractive old lamps and cut-out rocking horse sign still displayed outside **Linney's shop, 13-15 Lake Street, Leighton Buzzard** (SP 922250) amidst all the redevelopment in that area.

Dunstable

Another distinctive sign is to be seen above **Charlie Cole's cycle shop, 20 High Street North, Dunstable** (TL 018219). It is a genuine penny-farthing bicycle complete with an immaculately dressed miniature rider.

Sutton

From an earlier age of travel is Bedfordshire's only **packhorse bridge at Sutton** (TL 221474). Dating from the 14th century it was just wide enough to take a loaded packhorse, but modern motor vehicles are forced to use the ford alongside.

Cople

On the road between the Great North Road and Bedford (A603) is the former **tollhouse at Cople** (TL 104493). Once there were over 30 such tollhouses in the County, but now only one other example survives (at Bromham, on the road to Stagsden). In the 18th and much of the 19th century, the main roads were run by Turnpike Trusts who charged all travellers a toll to pay for repair and maintenance costs. The Cople tollhouse dates from about 1770 and the toll collector would have sat in the front porch to look out for approaching travellers.

Sandy

The Great North Road (A1) was a favourite haunt of cyclists, and just off the present road is this charming little **memorial garden to Frederick Bidlake, near Girtford Bridge** (TL 163487). Bidlake began his cycling career in 1883 and went on to establish many cycle and tricycle records before becoming President of the North Road Cycling Club. Since the Club started many of their races and trials from Girtford, this spot was chosen to commemorate Bidlake after he died in 1933.

Linslade

The Railway Age first impinged on Bedford-shire when the London and Birmingham Rail-way was opened in 1838. This line involved the construction of **Linslade Tunnel** (SP 918261) and at the northern end, which is visible from the Leighton Buzzard to Bletchley road (B488), modern inter-city electric trains suddenly come roaring out of these seemingly medieval castellated portals.

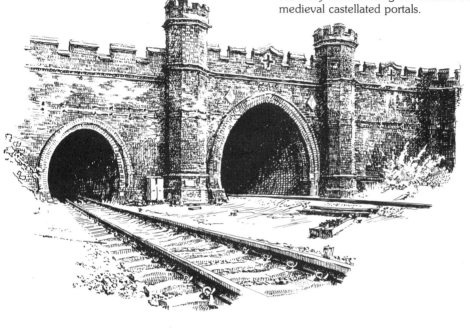

Southill

The man who did more than anyone else to encourage the spread of railways in the county was W.H. Whitbread, and he was an active promoter of several local lines. A ***stone obelisk at Southill*** (TL 132419) stands on the edge of his family estate, beside the road from Old Warden to Ireland, and pays tribute to his efforts in these words:

> *To William Henry Whitbread Esquire*
> *For his Zeal and Energy in promoting*
> *Railways*
> *through the County of Bedford.*
> *1864*
> *Erected by Public Subscription.*

Cardington

The landscape south-east of Bedford is dominated by the vast **airship hangars at Cardington** (TL 079466), which are visible for miles around. These hangars are over 800 feet long, are nearly 180 feet high (Nelson's Column could almost be stored upright inside one), and over 270 feet in overall width. The main doors weigh 940 tons, are mounted on rails, and are operated by electric motors. The left-hand hangar was originally put up in 1916-17, but greatly enlarged to its present size in the later 1920s when the second shed was brought from Pulham in Norfolk.

By then Cardington seemed destined to become a major centre for international air travel, and the hangars housed the two giant airships, the R100 and the R101. The R101 was actually built at the Royal Airship Works, Cardington, but unfortunately in 1930 it crashed in France on its maiden flight to India, killing all but 6 of its 54 passengers and crew. This ended any further development of airships in Britain, although in recent years the Goodyear airship *Europa* was constructed at Cardington.

Potton

Perhaps the most interesting railway relic in the county is the **former railway locomotive shed at Potton** (TL 221489). It now stands in the corner of a market garden just off the Biggleswade Road. It remains largely intact in spite of the fact that it has not been used for its original purpose for over a hundred years. It was erected in connection with a light railway built from Sandy to Potton, by Captain William Peel of Sandy Lodge, at his own expense and entirely over his own lands. The railway opened in 1857 but by that time Captain Peel, who was the third son of Sir Robert Peel (the famous Victorian Prime Minister), had been posted to the Crimean War, where he gained the Victoria Cross. He was then sent on to India where the Mutiny had broken out, and he died there in 1858 from wounds sustained at the second relief of Lucknow, so sadly he never saw his railway in operation. It closed in 1862 when the Bedford and Cambridge Railway was opened and the engine shed has been used for other purposes ever since.

By remarkable coincidence, the small tank locomotive that was housed in this shed, "The Shannon", has also survived. Having been passed on to the Wantage Tramway, it is now preserved in full working order at the Didcot Railway Centre, Oxfordshire.